Still I love

ERISE AMADO

A Compilation of Poetry and Prose

DEDICATION

To all the women that came before me
and all the women that will come after me

We are proof that love can grow even
from places that hurts us the most

To my mother's heart
I pray one day you find love again

To my father's mind
I pray one day you find forgiveness

To my reader's soul
I pray you find love in between my words
and I hope they guide you to find it within too.

CONTENTS

Still I love

Preface: The Pain of Living

When I was a child, I used to avoid pain at all costs. Until I grew up and learned that one of the biggest catalysts of pain is the avoidance of it.

I avoided bikes, analysed the risks and probabilities of falling and skinning my knees or stumbling and twisting my foot, and wondered if I ever would crack my head open like the kid in fourth grade did. Little did I know about the depths of pain that I was yet to encounter. Little did I know that there were more ways to crack your head open.

My second fear was breaking a leg, but do you know what I learned that hurts more? Saudade. Saudade, a Portuguese word that has no translation in any other language, we've all had a taste of it at least once, that feeling that feels almost like losing a limb. A part of us.

Saudade of a love of the past that never made it to the future, Saudade of the friend that moved overseas, or the one that moved in heart and mind and you can't recognise them anymore. Saudade of those who left too soon, and we all know at least one or two. Saudade of my grandma's recipes. Saudade of the sand. Saudade of the sea. Saudade of what we once had and who we never had the chance to be.

All Saudade leaves are remnants, remnants of "use to be's" and "wishes it had been".
I learned that fracturing a bone hurts like hell when my cousin broke hers at my aunt's J wedding, but do you want to know what hurts like hell too? Love. Love is the biggest fracture of life. A hell of a drug. An extreme sport. Some analyse the risks and probabilities of falling, others just dive in, and even after every fall, no matter how long it takes, they are back up again, ready to fall again in the depths and promises of a true love. Every love leaves and takes a piece of us, some bring drama, others leave some trauma, and we don't know whether the next one will be worth the fall.

Some of us grew up in dysfunctional environments, stuck in toxic cycles and distorted versions of what love should be. So, we're afraid to love again. We're afraid to end up in the same place that once had broken us. And others are addicted to it.

This is how I ended up being the avoidant-dismissive type. The "I don't need a man type" or the "every man in my life will leave as they always do" type. Pushing away the people I loved the most with the fear of codependency or abandonment. Focusing so much on how others could ever love me and forgetting how to love myself. Self-sabotaging and unaware of all the trauma that was left for me to deal with.

Maybe it was never love, because love has no intention of causing trauma - I would think to myself. Love has to be more than broken hearts and fracturing bones, yet life is more complicated than that. Sometimes we hurt because we're hurt, or we can't help but love those that hurt us the most because that's the type of love we were conditioned to accept.

It takes a lot of deconstructing, reparenting, self-awareness and self-love to heal the fractures. It takes a lot of time for us to believe again that love can be more than broken hearts and broken bones.
Love can heal the deepest wounds, no matter how painful the past we can still choose to love and live a present where our past no longer hurts us, but it has to start with ourselves. Love is the most powerful force known to man.

Love is putting the pieces back together, it is healing, it is loving, understanding and accepting your flaws as if they were your best feature. Every love leaves and takes a piece of us, some, will even leave you better than they found you. And trust me, it will find you, you can lose it but it will find you again and again.

Because it is bigger than us, more powerful than everything else we'd have lived. With love, the fall has no dimension, no concrete intensity, no matter how severe the fracture, there will always be another two hundred and six bones in our human body to break.

There will always be two hundred and six ways to fall into or apart with it. The greatest pain of them all I would say, and so worth it. I wish someone would have told me that the biggest fracture would be learning how to love myself.

My third fear was my mum and a wooden spoon. So, I always behaved. Never took risks. Behaved until I learned that life has a different way to beat you up, with disappointment and regret. That the biggest risk in life is not taking any risk. Because everything heals, the fractures, the cracks, the scars, everything, but the regret of not trying.

The guilt of not staying true to yourself. The pain of regret is worse than the pain of failing and falling. The regret of losing love out of pride, the regret of not reaching out to that friend that moved overseas, the regret of not tasting my grandma's recipes before she died, the regret of not saying goodbye to those who left too soon, the regret of not following my dreams and giving myself a chance to be who my inner child wanted to be. The regret of not giving love a second chance, of loving with all I had to give out of fear of being hurt. The regret of never learning how to ride a bike. And finally, the regret of never publishing a book, so here we are.

- always with love, Erise x

Saudade: noun [soh-dah-duh] European Portuguese: is a deep emotional state of nostalgic or profound melancholic longing for an absent something or someone that one cares for and/or loves.

1 CHAPTER

"And still it hurts"

Poetry

Every time I seeked for love

Every time I seeked for a safe haven

arms to embrace me and protect me

but never had the chance to grasp it

Every time the silence consumed me

Every time I thought I wasn't good enough

good enough to be heard, seen or loved.

Every time I thought life wasn't worth living

Every time I seeked for myself

and couldn't find me

 poetry found me.

Broken bonds

First love often comes with a first heartbreak
although I thought we were meant to touch eternity
to be bonded forever like normal families do.
The first heartbreak often comes
 from those that should have loved us unconditionally.
Bone of my bone
Flesh of my flesh
Hoped that our blood were thicker than
the circumstances that tried to dilute us
Prayed that I would wake up one day and
find out it was all a lucid dream
only to wake up to the reality
that my first love had abandoned me
Bone of my bone
Flesh of my flesh
Blood of my blood
You taught me
all of this doesn't matter
you taught me that
blood ain't thicker than water.

Father

There is always a void attempting to be filled
 with past memories and resemblances
A broken figure supported by imagery and language
broken shards falling one by one,
day by day until there is nothing else to sustain.

Until I stop seeing you in the arch of my smile
and hearing you in the calmness of my voice.
Until I stop seeing you in my brother's facial expressions
until we stop having the impression that he is you in person
 until my mother stops stating that I am your distorted version.

 Until there's nothing else to sustain
until there's no trace of you to maintain.
There is always a void attempting to be filled
 with memories that no longer exist.
I find myself sometimes looking for you
in places you have never been,
in pictures that have never been taken
and in objects you never touched.

I am sorry the world broke you
 and you had to break us too.
I still seek for you in every man in my life
and I wonder if they could ever love me
 the same way you once loved us.
Yet I still avoid your resemblance in every man I meet
because I wonder if they will leave me
the same way you did.

Remembrance

Remember the body where you once found your home, the same body we both cohabited in different dimensions, the body that your eyes saw almost bleeding to death, so it could bring life to me.

The same body you cried out to God to not be abandoned by its soul when my mother was taking her last breath. Remember the sheets drenched with blood, and I, a new-born crying in the cold, remember that particular moment when you realised that everything you ever loved, would be everything you once lost.

Sometimes I wonder what if the five minutes came and my mother could not be saved? I wonder if you would have stayed until now. Other times I wish that twenty-two years ago my mother had stayed home that night and never had met you. As twenty-two pounds of agony leaving her shoulders. And although I would not be present, neither would be the scars she tries to cover every day. Neither would be the feeling that everything I ever loved, is stuck in a man I forever lost.

- unsent letters to my father

Homebound

I wish I was homebound
Bound to a place where every step I take doesn't feel this heavy
As if I am carrying a weight I obliged myself to carry.
Wandering from place to place, from person to person
When will I ever find home?

Searching for fuel to ignite a fire that will never burn me enough.
Incessantly searching in others what I can't find in myself.
I crave a home, a place I know can return to.
I locked myself out of my body and swallowed the keys.
Since then I have been a nomadic
I'd rather be the one that leaves first than the one who gets left.
I am tired of being the one who gets left.

After spending sunrise after sunrise, moonlight after moonlight,
 painting and retouching, refurbishing and decorating.
 All to make them home, all to make them mine.
Until the walls start cracking
And this person that you once called home
Says that they don't love you anymore.

It was then that I understood why
you can't make a home out of people.
It will come a day when you wake up
and realise that you're homeless.

gut feeling

the sea washing away the sand
the last seconds of your favourite song
memories slowly blurring
the absence in your presence
the distance look and hollow voice
I saw you dissipating
right in front of my eyes
everything slowly fading
slowly blurring into that wrenching feeling
those five words that haunted me for weeks
as your love slips right from between my fingers
those five words come as affirmation that
you don't love me anymore.

Worse days

I've had better and worse days, although they all seem to mesh into one.

Right now, I am sitting on my worst days. My body is perfectly moulded to my bed after all the sleepless nights and days spent stuck in it while reminiscing about you. Finding reasons why my love wasn't enough for you when I overextended myself for you. Exorcised all your demons for you. Thinking I held the antidote to your toxicity. Hoping I could heal you.

Every morning I wake up with the same feeling of emptiness and nothingness. Stuck. Stagnant. You left a void in me and it feels like nothing else can fill me.

Damaged goods, why couldn't you leave me the way you found me?

I was full of life before you came in, so in love with myself before you loved me, the best version of myself before you ruined me. You changed me so much that I can't find myself amongst all the other versions of me that I created to please you.

All the pain concentrated in my gut, the same gut that once betrayed me. I hated that I was wrong about my gut being right. I haven't eaten for days and thought about putting an end to this in so many different ways. How do you mourn someone who is still here? Alive, breathing, living their lives like nothing had changed? When should you say your farewells? Where do I bury your ashes when parts of you still follow me everywhere I go?

The truth is I've had worse days, I won't let you take another credit from me.

Erise Amado

I count the months

it all seems so long.

Moving on seems so far away.

I blame myself for remembering and,

I blame myself for starting to forget.

- how long do I have to stay heartbroken?

Tell me

The phone doesn't ring anymore,

and I try to fight the urge to call you.

You made me feel like

I needed you to validate my existence.

I know I don't, but I have.

I've became too small next to you

and I used that to measure my worth.

Isn't love meant to make us blossom?

Isn't the right one meant to make us

fall in love with ourselves too?

So, tell me, why was it that the more I loved you,

the less I loved myself?

Ajar

There are days that I leave the door ajar, sit at the edge of my bed and wait for you to come back. Others, the sleep jettisons me, yet my subconscious stays alert waiting for the creak of the door to wake me up.

Some days, I hide under my bed, still, quiet, anticipating your return. I suppose that my persistence, my anxiety suffocates you, so I give you space, but my head stays revolving around you.

There are days I spread a trail of objects around the house because I know you hate disorder, so I wait for you to pick them up one by one until it takes you to me. I spray your favourite perfume, cook your favourite meal in hopes that the smell will trigger memories that your sight can't bring. I leave several voice calls. Perhaps your ears can long for a voice that speaks a language that only your body could understand. But these days, the tears touch my face before your hands can. Because the creak is never heard and I end up falling asleep under the bed, still, quiet, anticipating.

Perhaps my persistence, my anxiety suffocates me first, and the space I gave you will never be enough. The objects remain intact around the house. The plate of food remains untouched. The door never opens. And so, my heart. The bed remains empty.

And so, do I.

Still I love

Does it hurt more because they left,

or does it hurt more because you can't *let them go?*

Remnants

You have left yet you're still here
memories of you rolling in and out of my bed
breathing on my neck
biting on my lips
whispering into my ears
your taste lingering in my mouth
fingerprints sinked into my skin
you have left yet you're still here
I am sorry you're still healing from the darkness in you
and I'm sorry you missed the light in me.
I did not break with your departure
 because you left with bags well packed
ready for the world with an eagerness
that was never present when it came to me.
I should have known,
that those bags that you so proudly carried,
would not have had enough space
to fit the size of the woman I am
And I wish you had the decency
to take the memories with you too.
Now I am mourning for my fingers,
that will unconsciously reach for soft curly hair
 and never find you.
for my skin, that will eternally wait for teeth and warm flesh
 and never feel you
mourning for a body
that will insanely seek for a home that isn't you.
you have left yet you're still here.
I did not break with your departure.
It only broke me when you left and tried to take the hope with you.
the hope that I am also capable of being loved
and how naïve was I, to think that being wanted,
could ever be the same as being loved.

Grief holds me close for a few days. I take refuge in the same bed you once were too in love with me to leave, your scent remains there, along with all the other things you left in it. I wait for the mornings to come, but the daylight never sees me, and it seems that tomorrow will never come. I always say to myself, *tomorrow I promise I will hold onto strength, tomorrow I promise that we can start again. Tomorrow I promise not to give up on myself,* but it seems that tomorrow will never come for me.

My heart thinks that he'll be back.

Will you tell him, or should I tell him?

- conversations with the mind.

Empty promises

I promised I'd stop writing about you. I'd stop with the love songs and the letters. I'd stop with the visits to the past and the wishes that one day you'd stop by. Our time, my love, doesn't belong to the future we dreamed of. Our past, my love, had never prepared us for a future where we had to say goodbye.

I promised I'd stop re-reading past conversations. I'd stop reading between the lines, trying to locate at least a fraction of truth in your lies. I will stop writing about you. Delete the photographs that we took. The portraits we painted of people who no longer exist. I promise. I will stop.

Maybe not today. Maybe another day. And maybe, this way, I will keep on hold all the promises that I wasn't strong enough to let go. I keep going back and forth. Told you to leave but never slammed the door. You'd give me reassurance and valida-tion, but I was always insecure. I promised I'd stop calling your phone every time the alcohol found a way to run in my blood and, although you'd pick up, I know you would have let your pride speak first. I would try to find a hint of hurt in your voice and, like every other time, there would be nothing there for me to find. Only that broken and restless voice that you have after two or three rounds. I wonder if she knows about me. I wonder if she does it like me.

I promised I'd stop painting pink dreams that no other water-colour will ever be able to paint again. The brush is crooked, they say. The canvas is stained, others say. And even so, I still made beautiful art out of you. I promised I'd stop writing about you, but the ink hasn't run dry yet. And the memories haven't left me yet. Maybe tomorrow. Maybe another day, I'll stop writing about you.

It's not you, it's me

There is this lump in the back of my throat that prevents me from swallowing your words. Mouthful of sweet and sour promises you coerced me to ingest. It is not you, it is entirely and solely me, you said. It is the several other women I fantasise about, but not you. There is this chapter I am so eager to read but I cannot find the perfect character that you could portray. It is the future I want to create and cannot picture you in it. It is the time that is wrong, the circumstances, the distance to see you is too long. It is the universe. Your Venus in Taurus is not compatible with my sun in Gemini and, although I do not know what that means, I promise, it's still not you. Then you ask me if we can be friends and expect me to swallow that too. As if nights before I had not swallowed life out of you. As if I was not the centre of your fantasies, as if you never said that there would not be a future if I could not exist in your present. As if I formerly was not the main character of your book.

It is not you, you say.

Yet, it is everything else you want, *I am just not it.*

Half doses

You chose to make a home out of someone that isn't me and, here you are asking for shelter. To rest your feet and have a cup of tea, recharge your feelings until you find someone better.

To give me half love, half affection, half of you and expect me to be content?

When did I give you the impression that my love was for rent?

Chemistry

Your breathing near my neck creates an electric current
that travels down from my head to the sole of my feet.
I can see the satisfaction in your eyes.
Taste the ecstasy in your mouth.
 "Why do you feel so good?" you whisper in my ear, your voice
echoes in my mind, feeding my little ego.

"You know, we have great sexual chemistry, you can't deny" you
tell me, and I chuckle at the thought of it.
I know I can't. I think to myself and sit straight in silence.
The tension is real.
A magnet field that connects me to you, that makes my body
fervour for you, drenched in sweat and fluid, breathless. Always
imploring for more. And I want more.
Always more. A "more" that I discern you are not capable of
giving. There is always more.

There is a part of me that asks for your embrace, that seeks your
lap.
Fingers that take the strands of hair out of my face and wipe
my tears... that caress and that kiss the places that hurt the
most in the moments that I need the most.
 There is always more. But love with you is always less.
There is always that part that yearns for your mind to plunge
into mine with the same passion that you plunge inside me.
There is always more.I crave chemically, physically, biologically,
philosophically, and spiritual love.

I crave an undeniable connection. The spark everyone talks
about. The love story Shakespeare would have wished he had
written about.

I dream of a life beyond the one we have created in closed
doors. A sea of discoveries and adventures, of learning and
teaching.

I yearn for shoulders capable of carrying the weight of a woman like me, capable of enduring the days of flood and nights of drought, a voice that calms the waves of my insecurities.

I want your teeth to take my panties off.
Slowly, engaging, anticipating.
And devour me when you come back home from work.
I want to taste you while you tell me how your day was.
I want to make promises of love with your head glued to my chest.
To be the one that makes things right even when everything turns left.
I want to lose sleep talking about nonsense, about dreams or the last thread of hope we have placed in humanity.

To be the first thing your eyes contemplate in the morning and the last thing your mouth has the pleasure to taste at night.
I want that space that you store under lock and key in your heart. To be your muse, canvas, your gallery of fine art. To be the answer to the questions you've been afraid to ask. I never thought that finding someone to love me would be such a hard task.
"We have great sexual chemistry, indeed." I finally break the silence.

"But if there is something I learned with chemistry is that no reaction takes place without a substance, and that love, we don't have."

Back and forth

I have been trying to find excuses

to leave you behind

but you keep coming and going

sailing and roaming back to me.

This time I promised I would close the borders

to my heart, you have become a foreigner.

because you keep loving and hurting

and I keep crying and forgiving

because I got lost in the translation

of the love I thought you were giving.

 How do you manage to be the curse and the healing?

Still I love

You always crawl back to me

and I always run to forgive you.

Damage

How do I blame you for breaking me over and over again?
If I am the one who collects the broken shards,
and places every single one of them onto your hands,
expecting you to fix me?
Pretending that you have the power
to put the pieces back together.
Believing that the same hands that broke me
can make me whole again.

Still I love

I can't live in the present when my past is always visiting me
like an old friend I yearn to see.

Perfect mask

My mind became a tangled mess

Knotted around my fears

Wrapped around my pain

There's no way to untangle it

I can't ask you to pull the string

There is no way for you to find it

I have mastered camouflage

I always wear the perfect mask

Same hands

she sought solace in the same hands she found ache

hands that pledged commitment

that held her waist gracefully

that drew her close gleefully

were the same hands that condemn

that drew her close to an abyss of sufferance

that made her life a mayhem.

would she have known

would she have hidden in guilt or shame?

if the hands of a victim

and the hands of an abuser

appeared to be the same?

Rollercoaster

The highs are so high

The lows even deeper still

A rollercoaster

In the madness, we,

Find ourselves lost and broken

Yearning to be free

But you won't let go

And I won't let go

None of us can set each other free

We look for danger

For we never knew safety.

For love is meant to be a bird, with you, it was its cage.

Lucky you

Lucky you that I still don't know my worth
Lucky you that your love engulfs me
and the thought of life without you gives me anxiety
Lucky you that I don't know what I deserve
Because I never had better so I settle for worse
Lucky you that I still want you
When all you do is cause damage to my soul
When love is meant to expand and all you do is diminish
When *I love you* only ever leaves your mouth
Every time I threaten to leave
Lucky you that I still don't know my worth
because every time you say you'd change I'd always believe

Some people can't fathom

the idea of a healthy love

because they haven't experienced it themselves.

It is hard to be what you don't know

Just like the others

How do you know if it is love or

the idea of being in love that trapped you?

I wonder if this feeling of high is merely masked

by a high low that is yet to come.

I wonder if it is the affection I never had,

or the attention I always craved,

the good part of me I saved,

for the good one

for the right one

for the I will show you

I am not like the others one

Just for time to show me, that maybe,

you're exactly like the others

just a little less chaotic

a little less toxic

but the damage that you cause is exactly the same.

Abandonment issues

They come and go

and I watch them leave

one by one, memory by memory

what we could be

what we had potential to be

memories come and go too

they never leave when they leave

and I watch them play in my head

over and over again

why did I allow them to use and misuse me?

because they come and go

and I watch them leave

I never believed anyone would come and stay with me

Infatuation

Infatuation is the new tendency

looking for passion in sore hearts

getting pleasure in thirsty bodies

filling space with more gaps

being in love became a hobby

leaving you first wishing you had stayed

we're here to play without being played

waiting to receive what you have not been given

but all you had received has been misgiven

placing me below, and raising you above

mixing sugar with salt

shedding blood and calling it love

Anxiety

Words don't come effortlessly; they cluster upon my tongue, too heavy to be lifted, too dense to be swallowed as if I had a lump in my throat made by all the things that I left unsaid.

Sometimes I find myself running in circles, over and over again, left and right, up and down, and more often I go through the downs.

As if this narrative never really reached its conclusion, as if the character of this book lived in a loop, full of uncertainty, doubts, and hopeless delusional moments. Caving holes whenever she goes, filling them with nothing but more hollowness.

Heavy streams of feelings I no longer feel are still stuck in this dark grey matter that I no longer listen to, but it keeps storing all the memories, and all these emotions that walk hand in hand with them.

Where a huge network of nerve endings and touch receptors keep reminding me that the pain is still there, yet is all psychological, and if you ask me to point where, how can I point to everywhere?

I wonder how one can be so stuck yet moving, so small yet engulfing, so simple yet dense, so certain yet still not making any sense.

Invisible

I dressed myself to the thoughts of you undressing me

brushed my hair to the feel of you fondling me

applied gloss on my lips wishing that you could taste me

The men in the city eat me with their eyes

 their starvation fills my stomach with guilt

because how can I lower myself so much

to base my self-worth on someone

who doesn't even acknowledge my existence?

Potential

It's difficult for me to assimilate the complexity of lost souls. Those who wander through empty avenues and chaotic roads, those who get constantly lost in the labyrinth, those who decide to emerge from the abyss or fall into it, and those who try to find themselves.
And then there's your type, the ones who choose to be lost. Sometimes I compare the fragility of glass and the fragility of a house of cards.

Broken shards spilt on the floor, cards spread all over.
I could pick up all the cards on the floor, the ones hidden under the sofa next to an empty bottle of rosé you let me have the last sip,
and even the ones behind the counter where I cooked your favourite dish.

And I thought I was capable of picking up the broken shards, one by one, piece by piece and gather them all together.
That was my first mistake.
I saw you like a structure made of glass, hoping that I could put your pieces back together, and design it how I wanted like a house of cards.

They are gone with a blow and built again.
So frail yet manageable.
I was unaware of the crystal particles and lost broken pieces. I've forgotten how the particles of dust were what made you who you were.

I led you to a type of assimilation even I couldn't assimilate. That was my second mistake. Trying to glue you in a type of shape and dimension you weren't by nature, trying to make you a whole, for you to fall again and be left in halves. Attempting to turn you into the type of man you dreamed yet feared to become.

You turned me into a lost soul wandering through your empty avenues and chaotic roads, trying to kill the demons of a soul who doesn't want to be found and saved.

I'm still trying to assimilate how abruptly I let myself be consumed by you, by your demons, so attached to your roots.
I got lost in my own complexity trying to find yours. Compensating your lack of self-love by giving you mine. I can't do that for you.

That was my third mistake, thinking I could be capable of helping you get your shit together, put your pieces together. You're broken by nature.

My biggest mistake was that I didn't see the person you were,
I saw the person you had the potential to be.

Parallel love

I guess I thought love would happen that fast

with a stranger I gave a second glance

or with a guy on bumble

such perfect match

butterflies would start their ecstatic motion

pulse rates would increase

and in two seconds I would have fallen in love with them

and they would reciprocally have fallen in love with me

then the timid smiles and soft hellos,

the dates and sad farewells

but love doesn't happen nowadays

 we simulate it.

Thirst men

For them, our body is a vacancy

a journey with no destination.

a battlefield for decency and blatancy

their option for relaxation.

They come to us with

a thirst that never ceases,

a hunger that never contends

edacious fingers looking for a waterfall

that should never flow for them.

The real you they say

"I want to get to know you, the real you." - They always say.
Yet they're selective, they prefer to touch the parts of you that are
less prone to break. To be the type that does not want to give as
much as they want to take.

Addicted to your highs, repulsive to your lows.
Will they ever be able to see you naked, without taking off your
clothes?

"I want to get to know you." - You say. Yet you can't even pro-
nounce me correctly. The consonants of my name cannot make
love with your native language. The vowels of my surname fight
against your vocal cords. You're not familiar with names that carry
their own baggage. Thirty minutes into the date and I want to
shrink in this chair and vanish.

You're already fetishizing about me calling you Papi. For the
one-hundredth time, I'd have told you - I speak Portuguese, not
Spanish. *"I want to get to know you, for who you are."* - You say.

Attempting to pull on my heartstrings, but your focus is in the
hive between my legs that you're so eager to feast on. You hope it's
worth the sting. They say that the way to a man's heart is through
his stomach. And I heard you have the most exquisite palate.
Thus, I'm afraid if I open myself to you there will be a lot on your
plate.

Will you separate the flesh from the bone? The mind from the
soul? The half from the whole? The self from the love? The chem-
istry from the spark? The ass from the stretch marks? The past
from the trauma? The present from the karma? The scars from my
ex? Or the trust issues that came next?

"I want to get to know you, the real you." You say, but you're se-
lective. You prefer to touch the parts of me that are less prone to
break.

First timers

All I ever wanted was to be someone's first
First choice or first lover
First thought in the morning as they awake
First lover that ever made them feel this way

All I ever wanted was to the chosen for the right reasons
Not when you're 12 and boys tell you they want
you to be the first black tits they see
Not when you're 16 and they tell you're not their type but
 you're the first black girl they find pretty

Not when you're 20 and become the first that fulfils their fantasies
I have been the first but for all the wrong reasons
I want to be first that transforms you into poetry
The first that makes you mind race and lives rent free in it
The first that you explore the world with

All I ever wanted was to be someone's first
Out of question, not a circumstance,
not a lucky coin you randomly found in your pocket.
I have been the first for many reasons
The first that is always placed last.

Reciprocity

You keep giving and giving

Pouring it all

You keep filling others,

And you?

Who will fill you up?

There are some people that we should leave in the past where they belong, where they were left, where we were left. We don't realise how damaging it is to still crave to be up to date about their present, still dreaming about their past and wishing for a conjunct future.

Having this urge to know how they're coping, how they're breathing, especially when they are doing so well, and you're the one struggling to take in some air, it's unhealthy. Leave them where they were left.

  - block them

Still I love

That bittersweet taste still lingers in your mouth

You try to gargle it away, kiss it away, spit it out

The scars painting your skin from north to south

You say that it does not hurt anymore,

That time is your healer, not just a reliever

Let me see them, kiss them better, blend them better

I know you're still hurting, I know it's still burning.

Let me take the pain for the two of us.

Rotation

My mother's friend still mourns for a love long gone, for a love that is dead but still perambulates here. She's prisoned in grief, in memories and in her idealism.

My mum tells her to move on, he has moved on. This is what everyone says, although, it should not be up to the other person's movements to make us move. Because we rotate and rotate and remain there, rotating around them.

Their movement makes us rotate and we aren't aware of how this makes us their satellites. Rotating from grief to memories, from memories to expectations. And when we realise that our expectations cannot be met, we return to grief.

You must escape this pattern. You must exit the orbit. Rotating does not equate moving on.

You'll always return

To grief

To memories

To expectations

And your expectation never revolves in leaving the orbit.

"Time heals everything", they say.
And you wonder if your clock ticks
slower than everyone else because it still hurts.
You count every second,
every moon phase that goes
every season, every birthday.
Every moment relied on the promise
that tomorrow will heal you
Only time itself doesn't heal emotional wounds
Time conceals them.
Just like when you take a paracetamol to ease the pain
your body blocks the sensation of pain
but the headache is still there
Stinging.
Time doesn't heal everything.
You just don't touch your wounds
As often as you used to.

Closure

We say we want closure
but can't close that door even
if there's nothing behind it.
Closure comes when you want it to come.
It is not a voice or a text notification
When you see them looking their best
or looking for the one that comes next.
Offer yourself the peace of closure.
We say we want closure
When all we want is a different outcome.
When all we want is for them to come back
and shower us with rose petals and apologies.
To hold us and never let go
but it is time to let go.

Let them go.

We insist on making people stay for the wrong reasons.

Stay

We stay many times for the wrong reasons when we have every reason to leave. *"You should leave him, you should move on"*, your friends say. And I swear that I closed the door, I deleted and blocked contact, and I tried to create boundaries.

I removed myself physically, but I could never really leave mentally and emotionally. Part of me had my foot on the door because I was afraid that door would never open for me again. Sometimes we look for all the reasons to leave the in other person, hoping that everything will change, that this time will be different. Still, the hardest part is to find that reason within ourselves. We often stay not because we can't leave that person, but because we can't abandon ourselves.

The hardest part when you leave is letting go of the person you used to be when you were with them. Where do you leave the plans that were left unfulfilled? The house you could have bought and the memories you would have created in every corner of that house that was left to be built.
The hardest part is to let go of the potential of what could have been. We stay because we are unable to let go of that familiarity. We stay because we want to feel that we still belong. The hardest part is to let go of that routine, and you find yourself folding your shirt the way they used to do it or make that coffee in the morning the way they used to love it.

Oh the hardest part is to stop thinking that no other embrace will feel the same or that no one will ever see you the way you felt seen or love you the way you felt loved.

We hold onto the familiarity and the comfort even if it isn't good for us anymore. We often stay because we don't want to leave that part of ourselves behind, that person that took us so long to become, if we decide to close the door, where do we leave them?

Goodbye.

I am not saying goodbye to you.

Forgiving, forgetting and letting go

Never really involved you

I realised that moving on was harder because

I couldn't forgive myself

I couldn't forget who I was

I couldn't forget what I could have done

What we could have been

I couldn't let go.

I finally know why it has been so hard to move on.

It's not you, it's me.

I had been afraid of saying goodbye.

I've been afraid to let go of the person I was

When I was with you.

To the ones I wish I loved enough

To V.

Sometimes I wish I had someone to talk to
but my throat has been swollen for days.
Nothing comes up, nothing goes down
I am still chewing your death in my mouth.

Mind numbingly, heart-rendering, gut-wrenching.
It is asphyxiating, intoxicating, excruciating.
Intolerable, incomparable, unpalatable.
Like someone jettisoned my appetite for life.

I hear "I am so sorry for your loss "every other day.
What did I even lose, what am I even meant to say?
If I had put you in the back of my mind to make it okay
To make it smoother to digest and easier to compress
If it wasn't too difficult for me to address
 maybe my mind wouldn't be in such a mess.
And I thought if I repressed my emotions
the lack of notion would make it hurt so much less.

I was never really good at expressing my love on paper.
So I seek comfort and for you in the form of prayer.
It works. At least I like to think so.
 I like to think that I am not going crazy
so I make everyone else look crazy instead.

 I like to think that my words build bridges for people to cross
but I hate to think that I only do it out of fear of being left
alone with my thoughts.

Sometimes I wish I had more time to talk to you.
And now I wish I just had someone to talk to.
But my throat has been swollen for days
Nothing comes up, nothing goes down.
I am still chewing your death in my mouth.

At least once

We are at a junction with no intersection
I am sorry my compass doesn't point
to your direction anymore
I promised you an undying love
loved you during the day
loved you during the night
from the bottom all the way to the top,
from the beginning and I thought
I would love you till the end
I watched our love die from day to night,
from the top to the bottom
from its beginning
and its supposedly unending end.
but I loved you,
at least once,
I promise
I did.

To G.

If I could take a few steps back
I would return to the same old room
To those nights where we used to stay up at 4am
while I read my whole poetry collection to you

You've read these words before anyone
else ever read them, now I fear
Everyone will read this before you do

If I could take a few years back
I would go back to that year you told me that you loved me
that we should forget everyone and move on
but I was in denial and too afraid to say it back

I have been holding my breath for too long
biting my own tongue for too long
Imprisoning myself inside this invisible
 cage of comfort because you're the person
Who knew how to take me out of it

If I could take a few steps back
I would show you how my heart beats for you
How I still cheer for you
How I still pray for you
If I could take a few steps back
I would have chosen you.

Almost

You will always be that unpainted canvas, that poem I preferred not to publish, that red wine that I never got to taste. You will always be my favourite incomplete wish. My body still squirms with pleasure just thinking about what your hands could do to me, but I am satisfied with our "maybe", our "almost was" than the certainty that I would never be happy with you.

The certainty that me and you could never be – and that would have *killed* me.

Still in love

He calls you at 3 in the morning, hoarse voice, barely speaking and you barely listening, barely caring, because you do not care. Yet you picked up his phone call, once again. You cannot smell the cheap beer or dry rum, yet you know his mind is spinning, and you try to pretend you are feeling numb. You tell him that you will always be that open wound in his heart that refuses to heal, that stubborn stain that does not want to disappear, that pain that insists on being felt. You will be wrapped around his mind, and he will try to untwist the remnants of you only to make everything more tangled.

 He will taste the fruit of life and never appreciate its sweetness for the mouth that comes after you will always taste bitter. Different bodies will occupy the left side of his bed, yet that side will always feel empty and cold instead. He will try to find purpose, he will always search for love, but they will not feel like the home he had found in you.

Then he tells you that you will never find someone that loved you as much as he did. How is it love if the more you "loved" each other, the less you loved yourselves? You both urge to end the phone call, but instead, you are both sat waiting in silence, waiting for your pride to be exorcized from your bodies. The truth is - it will always hurt on both sides of the call, no matter who lies on the other side of your beds if you are still ghosts that haunt and whisper inside each other's heads, with one trying to convince the other that they're better without them.

> - *"they will never be happy without me"* the toxic things we say to comfort our hurt ego

"Not the right time, not the right day."

Love came in with thunderstorms, hurricanes and a haven,
it gave me the disease promising a cure, a little pain it knew
I would endure, ruined in a day, lavished me in the other. It
just came in. And I let it stay, gave my effort and time in my
schedule and before I knew it was part of me and all the things
I rescheduled.

When you fall in love in a time that is disconnected, you must
understand that time will always be time, but you cannot guar-
antee that love will always be love. There's always something
different in a way, from "since when you've became a coffee
lover?" to "is that really the person I've fallen in love with in the
past?".

That's my fear. I always fear what I cannot predict, what I can-
not measure, or what I cannot see or discuss. I fear that when
the right time comes, the only wrong thing will be us.

Another lifetime

There was a time, my love, that I believed that we were not meant for this world. We might need another lifetime, another dimension, another space. For the one that we have now has no space for us.

We are running out of time, we are running a race we already lost.

There was a time, my love, that I believe that not everything that is meant to run its course finds its way. Perhaps unintentionally, we will follow the same path. Perhaps unintentionally we will arrive in the same destiny.

Perhaps in another lifetime, in another dimension, in another space, we will be meant for each other, we will run our course, we will find our way.

From all the men I've loved before

Some men in my life taught me that
A man will treat you the way he wants to treat you
They never want a relationship
They're never ready
I am too sweet
I am too confident
I want too much
I am too good
I deserve better, they say
There's no time
And then I see them cracking bones
And engulfing themselves to fit other people in their lives.
I see them taking them to places I wish we went
Telling them words I've been waiting for months to hear.
Tell me how would I not think the problem was me?
I see them
Being the man, they are for them,
The type of man they never were for me.
Other men in my life taught me that
A man will treat you the way he wants to treat you.
They will be ready even when they thought they weren't ready
You will be the right amount of sweet
The right amount of confident
You will never be too much.
You will always be that good.
There will always be some time
And you won't have to crack bones
And shrink yourself to fit in their schedule
Tell me how you could think the problem was you?
You'll see them
Being that man for you
The type of man others couldn't be for you.

Law of conservation of energy

Everything is energy. Even heat, even love, let it be both. So, tell me, if heat is a form of energy that is transferred from a region of a higher temperature to one of a lower temperature, maybe I was too intense for you, maybe I was the hot food you couldn't handle in your mouth. Well, poor you. Or perhaps I failed to notice the toxicity in you. Feeding me in low vibrations so I could make you high with mine. This exchange of energy that you made me believe was balanced, but there wasn't any balanced equation in us.

When I was a glass half full pouring myself to someone half empty. To someone who made me believe I was the broken one instead. If the heat of a region is caused by the movement of its atoms and molecules moving faster, perhaps I moved too fast, and you weren't able to catch up. Maybe I loved you too hard trying to prove I was capable of building something that lasts.

If the law of conservation of energy states that energy can never be created or destroyed. Only transferred. Only transformed. I refuse to believe that you created the monster in me, and I refuse to believe you destroyed it.

All this time, I thought you were the catalyst that brought the self-destruction in me. The "no one will ever be able to love me like you did". The "I am so hard to love, no one can ever get this deep". That "no one will ever be able to see beneath this tough skin".

If nothing can be created or destroyed, perhaps you have not destroyed me. I might have turned into something else. Perhaps there's still some love left. Perhaps this glass can be filled up again.

The law no one teaches you is to remain the same after feeling everything you felt when you know you were full before they came but couldn't remain full once they left.

I am afraid when love does come,
there won't be nothing left of me

2 CHAPTER

"And so...it heals"

I have been at war with myself to give you peace.
- and this isn't love.

These days sleep is no longer sleep anymore

Sleep is an escape

Yet closing my eyes only makes me see clearly

The very thing I am trying to escape from

    - myself

Healing isn't linear and it is far away from perfect. Wounds will reopen. Wounds will close. When does one become completely healed? When does the box of triggers become completely sealed? I thought healing would just involve reading thousands of self-help books, meditating every morning, drinking two litres of water a day, planning a self-care day every Sunday, going out more often and sitting down twice a week with a stranger that asks you a million times how you feel today. Shadow work is never on the to-do list, I am used to putting a bandaid on my wounds and pretend they don't exist. Shadow work is like touching an open wound, stretching a sore muscle, picking up broken glass from your feet, mourning from the loss of parts of you that you never knew existed.

Revisiting the past when you barely remember it because you fought so hard against your mind to forget it. Unlearning past patterns while creating new ones. Writing letters to your inner child every now and then. Sitting down with your pain with no judgement until you find the source of it. Until you face it.

You cannot remove the bandaid before the wound is healed and you cannot keep it forever to avoid seeing the scar. Give yourself grace, patience and understanding. Heal at your own pace but keep doing the work.

I was too busy trying to love everyone else
during times I should have loved *myself.*

The upbringings of bruised love

You grow up watching romcoms
fantasising about what love must feel like
reading Nicholas Sparks love dramas
and wondering when yours will come.
But downstairs the story isn't much different
the drama that nobody talks about behind closed doors
when tables are turned
vases are broken
bodies are bruised and love is long rotten.
Maybe one of them drank too much
and the other had too much to say.
You grow up watching romcoms
fantasising about what loves must feel like
but downstairs the show is quite different.
Your mother gets home late juggling three jobs
your father is absent,
and your brother has lost the idea of
what having a paternal presence feels like.
You grow up watching romcoms
fantasising about what love must feel like
but downstairs the show isn't much different
except not much is happening.
Your parents barely notice you
your father gives you money and calls it love
your mother spends her nights drinking red wine,
falling asleep to the sound of a failed marriage.
And you grow up watching romcoms
fantasising about what love must feel like
to only end up in the same broken relationships that raised you.

Our first relationship with parent figures creates the foundation for every relationship we have. We mirror their behaviours or are attracted to the same dynamics as adults. Whether it is the love we received or the lack of thereof. We hold onto trauma that for years remains dormant or undiscovered but imprinted in our subconscious. We repeat what we know, and we are attracted to what is familiar. Healthy relationships are created through reparenting. You have to be the parent you never had and be the adult your inner child always needed. Don't hold onto guilt if you have ever fallen into the same dynamics or couldn't see the red flags. Forgive yourself and give yourself a chance to create your own story, we all deserve our own romcom.

Don't fall back into old patterns

Just because they're familiar

The best could be waiting

For you in the unknown

How to love

I am still learning how to love the ugliest parts of me
Still learning how to touch the tender skin
Still trying to bring out of me what I have always kept within
I am still learning how to love
I don't know where to start
I never know when to stop
And I am still learning how to receive it
There is no bottom to switch it off
Sometimes I wish love came with an instruction book
Or with a travel book
So I could be stouthearted on this journey.
I wish it came with all the warning signs.
With the "handle with care" packages
With biochemistry formulas that I could follow
With calculations that I could find the solution for
But life has a different way of giving instructions.
You have to take what is given to you
Make something out of it.
And hope that in the end - it all works
And I hope that in the end
Love will work for me.

How to forgive

I am learning to stop being so hard on myself
For the times when I did not know any better
When I hadn't experienced no different
When I thought I had no option
When I couldn't see clearer
I am still seeking forgiveness
For the times I was a stranger to myself,
Too busy mourning the past
For the times I had no boundaries
Always afraid to say no
Always ready to please
For the times time I chose silence over speech
For all the time I chose others before me
I want to forgive myself for the times
I forgave everyone else but me.

Most of us live haunted
by the inability of forgiving ourselves.
- *forgive yourself*

First of December

The beginning of the end of a beginning. I guess I can say the same for me. This lost boat sailing and sailing with no precise destination, with no precise coordinates, looking to settle in shores that aren't ready to receive me.

Still looking for a place to call mine, when I have this body that is the first home I know, yet it is the first place I turn my back on as soon as things get unsettled. For I wish to roam around sometimes, try being in different bodies, seeing with different eyes, being around somebody whose love for me shall never cease.

I realised that I am not ready to sail to your shores. Don't think I ever did, not sure if I ever will. Forgive me if when you find this letter someone else will be sailing to your shores, and I won't condemn you, or crucify you, or stop you.

I am in search of more meaning, of more light, of more healing, some insight.

I am in search of more peace, of more silence, since the grey matter in my head is so clustered. I am in search of more passion, of more love, of more kisses and some wishes I never granted myself. No motivations, so many temptations, I am sailing so far from who I am. I want to sail to a place so far away from everyone and please do not look for me. I shall come back. I am in the beginning of the end of a beginning so please respect my privacy, this isolation and this need to repress. I am sorry for all the confusion and all feelings I find so hard to express.

If your words were bullets would you wonder how many times you have killed yourself?

If my lips told you stories of bitter and sour trauma would you still try to taste them?

If my body was a pool of scars, would you still want to dive in it?

If my tears washed away all the shame I can't confess

Could my hands hug me instead of trying to hurt myself?

I am a boat with no destination, leave me alone to find my own.

The panic attacks never tell me when they're coming. Depression did but in different ways. They both whisper into my ear "what if tomorrow starts without you? No one will care".
Sometimes anxiety corrals me between four narrow walls that makes my every move unbearable, every breath excruciating, and I can't breathe.

I start thinking of how suffocating it would be to wake up on a morning when I wouldn't be awake. Listening to my mother's wails, the silent cry of my brother and the bitter taste of regret grabbing my father's neck with both hands, and I wonder which of the three would suffocate first. And I, on the other side, without being able to do anything, without being able to be the air and the referee who dictates how long is left for them to be able to breathe again. I start thinking of the love I never lived, the kisses I never gave, the I love you's I never said and the love that I never made.

I think of the hands that never touched me, the words they never told me and the proposal that never came. I think of the wedding dress that was never made, the career that I never started, and the children I never raised. Would it be a girl or a boy, would God even bless me with a fertile womb? I think about the pancakes I never made in the morning, the smell of my mother's cooking, the recipes I never learned and the mother that I had and could never be. The socks I'd find scattered around the house, every corner where I would have made love, the mornings with red wine stained on my shirt, stumbling on objects I wouldn't have remembered having placed there, and my children playing in the hallway, the type of normal life I would have loved.

But then it comes the anxiety, the panic attacks, insomnia, the disguised insecurity, the weeping and the cry for help that I never sent. And I try to breathe again. I try to be my own referee.
I try to bring a little oxygen. I try to get some calmness, mind-fulness, and love. I try to be the one who dictates that tomorrow should and will start with me, no matter what depression says to me.

Still I love

I don't write for the pleasure of writing anymore. I write because I want to exist. I want to know that I belong to the paper and the paper belongs to me, I want the reassurance that I pertain to the only thing that makes sense to me.
That feels like home to me.

- *journaling is therapeutic*

Stay a little longer.

"Stay a little longer", I really would like you to stay. Your glass is empty, I promise to fill it with a little more wine. For you, I pour everything. Stay a little longer, my bed is so empty, me and my depression are so used to sleeping in it all day, and I am dying for a night where I don't feel so lonely. Can you stay for another hour? Can you come and warm me up? The winter is slow, but I'm in such a hurry to feel warm skin against mine, or perhaps I drank too much. But stay a little longer. I don't want you to go like the others, today I just wish for fingers running through my scalp, and I'm in need of your lap. I really would like for you to stay.

We learn the real meaning of something once we experience the lack of it. So I thank the depths of sadness for the urge to experience the heights of happiness.I thank the times of solitude for teaching me how to be comfortable with my own company.I thank emptiness for showing me what being full and whole should feel. I thank the people that hurt me for being the example of who I shouldn't become.

And I thank you for showing me what love is not.

Lonely journeys

You can't build a bridge

And expect people to cross it and meet you there

Some people help you build it

Some people can't wait to destroy it

And others will never be ready to cross it with or for you

You cannot force them to meet you halfway

You cannot force anyone to meet you there

Heavy days and empty days
Yet the mind is always so full.
Some days you will try to get yourself busy
to distract your heart and mind.
Others, the anxiety will hold you tight
and your bed will sweet-talk you into
spending more time in it.

Sometimes when the world is falling,
we tend to fall with it too.
A quicksand
the more you move
the quicker you sink

Some days will be heavier than others
Or emptier than others
And the world may be falling
And your mind always so full.

Take time to breathe.
Find some quietude.
You don't have to fall with the world too.

Healing is an ongoing process, but it doesn't mean that the wounds won't close and the scars won't disappear and you will feel that pain again. Some wounds stay healed forever without scarring skin, you will pass your hands across it and won't remember that once that surface was tender. There is pain that disappears without you noticing. The thing with healing is that right after one wound closes, another may appear, right after one scar disappears another is forming and you might think you're not healing, you might think the pain will never go away. It is painful when life hits you in different ways and you find yourself having to place bandages all over you, it feels like you're starting all over again and it hurts a thousand times more.

my war is to find my peace

Co-existence

A part of me is noise

the other is silence waiting to be heard

A part of me is a crowd

the other is loneliness in search of company

A part of me is from the world

the other will never have who to belong to

Both parts of me coexist, never one-sided

After all, I am just a girl

 that was born in between the equator line

I was already born divided.

In between

They teach you that in this world
It is to eat or be eaten.
To hunt or be hunted.
To kill or be killed.
I thought this world would have created exceptions
That are not just black and white
Solely tea or coffee
Strictly left or right
And it feels like a punch in the gut
When they try to teach you that
There is no to love and to be loved
There is to be loved or to be broken
There's no in-between.
And it has been taking me years to realise
This is the world's undoing.
But it doesn't have to be mine.

Full course of hate

My stomach is full
There is so much greed and loathing
So much violence that we are being fed with
And I want to throw up

Rage, indignation and disgust
I try to digest, but it always comes up
For breakfast, I have bread and a cup of coffee
but the taste of iron lingers in my mouth
for the slaughter of my brothers and sisters
Whose bodies didn't even deserve to be put in a coffin.

For lunch, I am confronted with the rape
Wrapped up as false accusations and self-invitation
And no one talks about the human traffic
And the innocence that is ripped and forever gone.
I imagine the corpses of fathers and mothers
And children who never had the chance to be one

My tongue is asleep
but how can I keep silent
If throats are being cut
Let my voice be their loudspeaker
How can I keep silent?
If stories are untold
And deep white pockets are getting richer

For dinner, I am obligated to chew and swallow
The conformity that this world instilled
That tears will never be shed for the bloodshed
of my brothers and sisters
you can paint it all across their walls of
blind privilege but
they will never see us as equal.

"Oh, you're such a beautiful and smart black girl" someone once had told me when I was younger, but it wasn't a compliment, it was derision, cynicism, it was a punch in the throat that took years to hit me. And when it did, it hit hard.

In a world that teaches us to carry ourselves with pride, no guilt, no shame, my mother had to teach me that I had to carry myself higher, for I would have to carry more than I was accountable for.

And for every block I remove out of my way, they would place a thousand more.

"Beautiful" and I have to smile and swallow every phonetic spelling of it, they say it as if I was the right outcome of an anomaly. As if I was the lucky one. As if I did not deserve it. As if I quite made it to their beauty standard, but I was not there yet.

"Smart" but they could never accept me as the smartest in a class of white predominance or the one that expressed eloquently in their native language, the language that was never mine.

Shrinking myself to the idea that I was portraying this "educated" character just to be seen as less "black" than my counterparts.

"Smart", yet my mum told me I had to study the triple so that they could acknowledge a third of it. To stay away from the troubled black kids so that I wouldn't be categorised the same, yet I would always be the same, for they don't see trouble, they see black, and that's enough to be troubled.

"Smart" but not enough to know I was the "black friend" every white person claimed to have as an excuse for not being racist, because I always been "the different one".

"Black", they say it as if it was a life-threatening condition, a stubborn stain that doesn't want to come off no matter how much you scrub, and trust me I tried to, but it doesn't go.

In a world that teaches us to carry ourselves with pride, no guilt, no shame, tell me how can you teach a child that the colour of their skin is the heaviest weight they would have to carry for the rest of her life?

- *the weight of my skin.*

Black

I am a young **black** woman living in a world that undervalues all three.

I was born with a life sentence, hoping one day my words would set me free. But justice doesn't move with words, it moves with power, bloodshed, privilege, corruption, and deep white, rich pockets that are always the solution.

  As much as we continue speaking up, we're getting tired of talking. Talking to a system that asks for evidence, and we continue showing and we're tired of having to show proof; because the millions of testimonies aren't enough, the semen in our panties isn't enough, the hymen that was broken isn't enough, the blood in our belongings isn't enough, the pain in our speech isn't enough, the sequels that they leave isn't enough. But it's enough, we're tired. And we're tired of the trauma. The more we heal, the more we get tired of living in fear of being hurt.

 I mourn, I mourn for my sisters that succumbed to the silence, or those that were silenced. I weep for the little girl in me that had to learn "how to behave like a lady" from such a young age just to not fall in the whims of men. Because it would be my fault if my clothes were too tight or too short, if I smiled back, if I texted back, if I drank too much, if I told him to stop, or if I didn't fight back.

I am a young black woman living in a world that undervalues all three, in a world consumed by patriarchal standards and misogyny. I was born with a life sentence because the colour of my skin makes me a criminal, and my body makes me a victim who "invited" the abuser to come in.

I am a young black woman living in a world that undervalues all three. Still, before, I am a woman, before all that, I am human, and from human to human, when will you end my sentence, when will you set us free?

shrinkage

"You should wear your hair out more often."
The woman says, parting my hair in four equal sections.
"I would, but I hate the shrinkage."
The man comes and plants a goodbye kiss on my temple,
Then leans forward to plant another on hers, yet her body
tenses up.

The shrinkage.
But I am not talking about hair.
When he leaves, she tells me :
"My daughter, you have to bring the fire
to his belly and clearance to his mind.
Make sure the food is ready,
and your priorities are according to his time".

Here we go again, "how to keep a man chapter 2".
I have been submissive my whole life.
Submissive to becoming the best daughter, the best sister
Submissive to becoming the best woman.

The one that learns how to cook
The one that reads her books
The one that learns how to satisfy a man
The one that learns to control her hips
The one that opens her mouth
wide open to suck on his thumb.
The same thumb that I have to learn
 to be silent when it tells me to.

Shrinkage but I am not talking about hair.
And I am not holding my tongue.
It's swollen from all the times
I learned to bite on it instead of using it.

Still I love

From carrying the oppression of my women
Who shrink themselves to accommodate the big egos of their
men.
I am not holding my tongue.
Cut my throat open instead.

It is never "How to keep a woman"
because our women always stayed.
Shrunk. Compressed. Betrayed.
Bring the clearance to his mind, they say.
How can I be his peace and be at war with myself?

How can I sit in silence?
How do I make love with misogyny
And kiss the mouth that kisses
the butt of chauvinism and bigotry?

How can I iron his shirt while he's getting ready
 to be in someone else's bed?
The same shirt that will smell like sweat and hell
Covered in scarlet red lipstick when he
returns with it for me to wash it.

I can't clean the dust in the house and store
What's broken in me on a shelf.
To pour my heart out to everyone
Even if this means I'll forget to keep some to myself.

I wish I could tell that I am sorry you've been conditioned to this.
And your sister, and her sister, your mother and her mother.
Auntie, I am sorry this is the only form of love you had.
The only form of love you've seen
The only form of love you feel
The only form of love they taught you.
It has been taught from your father
And his father to his son and grandson.

This shrinkage.
This tough love.
This codependent love.
This abusive love.
This toxic love.
This everything but not love.

Because love isn't shrinkage
Love is an extension of everything you are taught
And everything you are given.

So let's teach our children better.
Give them something better.
Show them that there's better.

- *teaching my daughters how to take space*

Women

To all the women
Whose ribs cracked
You birthed nations
You built a community

With a soul of a thousand mothers
Heart soft like cocoa butter
You're the backbone
And more.
You nurtured the soil
That paved the way
To become the woman
I had dreamed one day.

To all the women
With jazz on their hips
And samba on their feet
You give life even if your soil is not fertile
You are committed and accomplished
Without a ring on your finger
Do not place your worth on the social construct
That makes you feel less of a woman

To all the women that empower other women
Whose shoulders I have cried
Whose finger pointed to the right direction
Towards self-worth
Towards ownership of my beauty
With no comparison
With no debasement
To all the women I saw cracking
Like walls of an old abandoned building.

You are worth healing.
You are worth loving.
You are worth the rebuilding.

- To all the women inside of me

Mirrors

Do you look for cracks in every glass?
Deflects in every mirror?
Reflection of who your mind fallaciously creates,
Every inch of you, you encounter an error?
Do you look for vestiges of every part of you
that once had broken,
Still hopeful of bringing them back.
Do you still scroll through your feed,
Comparing every other body that you see with yours
Or google how to remove your hip dips?
How to achieve that "skinny waist
But everything else is fat" silhouette?
How much is a surgery?
Since when did self-love become so expensive?
We're trying to love someone
Whose reflection in the mirror is not ours
And part of me is still trying to love
Versions that other people have created of me.

Self-love, self-care, and inner peace.

Taking care of yourself is also productive.

Dear Self

I still have so many things to figure out
So many obstacles to remove
So many open wounds to close
So many doors to open.

I am still learning.
I am still a learner.
Learning step by step,
Mistake by mistake,
Trials and errors.

Dear self, forgive me if I cause you a few bruises,
If I break a few bones
Or if I kill some of your time.
I am still growing.

Please understand if I act out of my character.
I am still learning how to correspond
my words with my actions.

Understand my need for space, my need for reclusion.
I am still figuring out what I need,
Figuring out what I want,
And frankly, figuring out who I am.

Surrender

There is beauty in surrender.

Surrendering isn't failure or weakness or the incapability of being good enough. You are good enough. It is about knowing your worth and accepting the present as it is. Let go with love and grace.

There is beauty in embracing the present moment, to find peace in between the pauses, in between the seasons, in between your breathing. Find comfort in the stillness. Holding tightly on what no longer exists or what we wish to exist only drives more pain.

Sometimes holding on hurts more than letting go.

And the greatest gift I could give myself after they left – was letting them go too.

Choose peace over everything

Remember that the way people treat you is only a mere reflection of themselves

People tend to project their subconscious insecurities onto others instead of acknowledging them.

And what you allow, persists.

amnesia

I find in scents

In places,

In touches

In unanswered questions

The wounds to heal.

Selective amnesia,

As I like to call

The brain blocks the memories

To help deal with the trauma.

As therapists like to explain

We pretend to forget the experience.

But the pain somehow never forgets to return.

The pleaser

There were times when I would break all my bones

Just to fit in that minuscule place you had left for me

I wish someone would have told me

I did not need to make myself small

To accommodate the desire of others.

I spent my whole life compromising for others
that I don't even know what I really want.

The next time someone asks me
"what are you looking for in a partner?"
I will skip the question.
When you tell someone exactly what you're looking for
It seems like they study you
and replicate every single thing you want to see.
They will tell you precisely what you want to hear.
They will take you to all the places you've yearned to go.
They will show you that everything you want,
you can find it in them.
Until they get exhausted of playing that character,
until that persona starts fading away
for you to see them for who they truly are.
And you'll find that they are everything,
But what you're looking for.

It isn't easy to get to know me entirely

because I always give myself in pieces

- *until I'm ready to give it all.*

Strength is also knowing when to give up
Recognising when something
is taking more of you than giving
doing more harm than healing.
Acknowledging that you deserve more.
There is also strength in walking away
from places you wish you could stay.

The only reason we want certain things is the feeling we believe we will get from having them. Once we get them, then we can be happy, we say to ourselves. And I wonder if it has been the same with me. Am I seeking for love to finally say that I am happy? Am I seeking for love or the feeling love gives?

Or am I seeking for love or the validation that I am worthy of it?

I wanted to tell you so much that I love you. I wanted to tell you that we did it, both of us. I wanted to tell you that over time things don't get any easier, there aren't fewer problems, there aren't fewer fears, but now we are stronger, more astute, and you know, the fall becomes less painful with you. I wanted to tell you that your scars are beautiful, they reflect your greatness, don't hide it. I wanted to tell you that now we love looking in the mirror, I love your reflection, I love my reflection, I love our body. I love to touch it, kiss it, feed it well, nourish it. I don't flinch that much when others try to touch me anymore. I'm sorry for the times we tried to hurt you. I wanted to tell you so much that not everyone is born a rose that is placed in a room, some are born sunflowers in the middle of the field, others are born dahlias in a flower bed. I wanted to tell you so much that I love you. Fully. And every day I water you, for every season we'll have reasons to blossom.

- letter to my inner child

Sabotage

This constant battle between

Not getting too attached

But not being too aloof

Not getting too close

But not staying too far

Not showing too much

But not being too unreadable

Maybe this the only way they won't hurt me, you think

But this is exactly how you end up hurting yourself.

Lost in this endless search to find someone who could love me
for who I am, for what I love, for what I see, for what I feel.
There would always be something that pushed them away.
Well, I pushed them away.
Because I knew that if it were me
holding the door wide open for them to leave,
it would hurt way less than watching them
pack their bags and walk away deliberately.
There are two types of people I have been searching for my
whole life.
The one that will remove my hand from the door
close it and will choose to stay,
and the one that will pack their bags
grab my hand and ask me to leave with them instead.

- the one that will stay

foundation

Understand that the relationship you have with yourself sets
a foundation for everything you relate to. To deposit trust
in others, start trusting yourself more. To feel secure in your
relationship, understand your insecurities. Be as kind to you as
you are to others. Before committing to anyone, learn how to
commit to yourself.

I am half drop, half ocean

half flower, half thorn

half soft, half stone

half lost, half found

half moon, half sun

half unpredictability

half consistency

but entirely me

Still I love

Affirm:

I am kind to the parts of me that are still learning, unlearning, and healing.

Allow yourself to be a beginner

Everyone has to start somewhere

Erise Amado

Purge

To evolve you need to let go of what no longer serves you

And walk away from all the things that are not

in alignment with your growth

Let go of old habits and break off toxic cycles

You have to remove what holds you back

Remove the anchor and set you free

Even if this means you'll be sailing alone for awhile

Be intentional, and you'll attract only what is meant for you

Still I love

Holding on what could have been doesn't change what was

How to let go and start healing

Allow yourself to feel every emotion
Allow yourself to grieve every loss
Understand that you are not what happened to you
Identify every pain without judgement
Mourn your past self
 and what you are still holding onto
You find closure once you accept
 the present moment as it is
Don't be reluctant to make space for something new
Letting go is also letting in

Learn to go and *let God.*

Self-ish

Don't apologise for choosing yourself this time

For putting yourself first for the first time

For establishing boundaries and drawing the line

It is selfish to give everything to others and leave nothing to yourself

I am not lost,

I am just not there yet.

Happy endings

Melancholic words flowed in between my tongue, quite bittersweet in my pen, nearly bleeding on my page. I have been yearning to feel something, because those feelings of nothingness, this emptiness that lives in my heart, this indifference that my mind convinced me to use as self-defense are failing to protect me from myself. I always believed that beautiful poetry only comes to me through hurt and darkness.

I always believed that happy endings only belonged in books, could only exist in fiction and, it could never be with the real me. All these characters would experience love but not me. A happy ending, just not with me. Until the day I accepted that warm sweet words could also dance in between my tongue, navigate through my body, moisturise my skin, bring hope to my pen and the kind of love these pages have been missing. Until the day I accepted that light could still come to me from a place of darkness and enter through the cracks of my bone.

In doubt, stay still

I am learning to trust and love myself entirely
To put the self-doubt to sleep
And on the days it wakes up
I will remind myself to stay still
Do you remember all the times
You thought you would never get through it, but you did?
For all the times you said that
You would never be capable, but you were?
I am undressing all the heavy layers
Exposing all my scars
I am healing and accepting the broken
And bruised parts of me that I have neglected
I will silence the self-sabotage
And on the days it gets too loud
I will remind myself to stay still
To mute the voice of the trauma
The one that kept saying that
I would never be able to love again, but I did.
The one that almost made me believe
There was nothing left of me,
But there is.

Sometimes things have to fall apart to fall into place

- meant to be

Stitches

I spent way too long stitching myself back together
Picking up the pieces, breaking down
the walls I spent a life building
Taking myself out to dates to get to know myself better
Watering myself so no grass is greener
like the one I grew within
For you to come like a tornado
with two legs and destroy me
When you heal, you outgrow the things
that are no longer aligned with your growth
There is no more space for what brings no value
It took time to deconstruct
what I once thought was best for me
It took too long to stitch myself back together
To just let anyone open my wounds again
And it can be a little lonely
Because now I know my worth and the value I bring
Now I know what I deserve and I won't settle for fragments
Loving myself properly can be a little lonely
but I am comfortable with my own company
I'd rather be alone than settling for a half-assed lover
Love me properly, love me louder, love me harder,
Love me better than I thought I could love myself
and maybe I'll let you in.

come in, but please,
remember to leave me the same way you found me.
-   *whole*

I deserve to be loved
I deserve consideration
I deserve reciprocity
I deserve understanding
I deserve appreciation
I deserve to be listened to
I deserve to be valued
I deserve love too

To remain soft after everything you've been through is a gift

Self-love isn't loving yourself at all times but rather choosing yourself at all times. It is learning. Unlearning. Letting go. It's hugging your best as much as your worst. Taking accountability for your mistakes without self-judgement and improving. To believe that no matter what you've been through, you deserve a chance to be happy. It's giving yourself a chance to be happy. Choosing yourself over and over again.

I used to only love myself on my good days.

See, your future is about the growth of your spirit and your soul. Connect with something deeper and that speaks truth to you. How you look, what you possess, where you came from does not dictate what your future holds. Do not place your value in life by how others see you or treat you. By who neglected you and rejected you. Move with love and compassion. Be authentic. Commit to your truth and what your heart craves the most. You are not what happened to you but what you decide to do with it afterwards matters. May God give you the peace and courage you need to trust that what is coming is way better than what is gone.

The barriers I've built in the past:

A rooted belief that everyone will leave me
A deep conviction that no one will be ready for me
I am hard to love.
Fear of overexpressing or under expressing my feelings
A deep feeling that I can never trust others.
Everything sounds too good to be true.

Removing those barriers:

Pour into yourself first.
Learning to experience people as they come, and as they go too.
Not everyone will leave you but not everyone will stay either.
Enjoy and honour every season of your life.
No one should make you feel like you're hard to love.
Don't be afraid to express your feelings.
Allow yourself to feel whatever you're feeling.
Trust issues generate more trust issues.
Deal with those first.
If it's meant for you, it will come.
What you seek is seeking you.
Believe that you are deserving and worthy of love.
It doesn't sound too good to be true, it is good, and it is true,
and you deserve every bit of that.

"Not knowing your worth will cost you a lot".

- *value*

Vulnerability

Vulnerability is beautiful. You wear your heart on your sleeve, you embody the things you feel, the things you see, the things you touch, the people you miss. You experience hurt the way you experience love, you can still learn from the darkness the same way you can learn from the light.

Vulnerability scares you because you don't know how to compartmentalise. Vulnerability has been breathing on my neck for years, right under my nose, waiting for me to show a part of me I've always been afraid to expose. My ears I've been weary of vulnerability. They say it's like putting the gun in your mouth hoping no one pulls the trigger, it is being naked in all forms that nudity can allow and still feel clothed.

My mouth has been avoiding vulnerability for years. I wondered why would I give someone power over me? What if they used my weaknesses against me? What if they pulled the trigger? What if they could never see more than just a naked body?

I failed to see the beauty and strength in vulnerability. In being open, in being transparent, in exploring my weakness as much as my strengths. In letting people in. I failed to see that being vulnerable doesn't equate to being fragile and prone to break. To give others the opportunity to break us. Vulnerability brings a sense of freedom I was depriving myself from feeling.

I learned that I shouldn't feel guilty for my vulnerability, my kindness or tenderness.

We tend to take life, people or even feelings for granted, as if they are supposed to stay here – on standby, untouched, unchanged.

I learned how everything is temporary – moments, circumstances, this chair I am sitting on, me and you. Us. And I learned to live every part of it for as long as it lasts. I will choose to love for as long as I exist.Openly, kindly, tenderly.

To my first love

Self-love
Should have been our very first love
Yet it is usually the one that comes last
Because we spend our whole lives searching in
Others what we think we can't find in ourselves.
The journey to self-love
To reconnection
To forgiveness
To acceptance
And growth
Is a lifelong journey
To love yourself is revolutionary
To feel so comfortable in our own skin
Embracing the beautiful and the ugly
The whole and the broken
The curve and the straight
The dark and the light
Allowing your body to tell the stories
It has been carrying for so long
From where it stretches and contracts,
To where it gives life to another life
To love yourself is revolutionary
Beneath the drama and the trauma
The fears, the scars, the tears
To love yourself is revolutionary
Despite the comparisons,
The unrealistic beauty standards
From how you should look to how you should behave
To love yourself is revolutionary
It is extra, more than ordinary
It is to feel confident
Sexy in my own skin
Proud of my own traits

It is to not feel too delicate
Or too strong
It is not to feel too quiet
Or too loud
It is to feel not too thin or too thick
It is to feel not too logical or too emotional
It is to replace self-sabotage with reassurance
To love myself is revolutionary
A woman that drown oceans
That empowers other women
That her beauty does not depend
or hide another woman's beauty
That makes space for others to take
To love myself is revolutionary.

Dear self,

I should have loved you in all the moments you needed the most and all the moments I thought you didn't. I should have loved you deeper like I tried to love everyone else. I should have loved you sooner, not when I thought I needed to be another version of myself that was more worthy of it. You deserved to be loved in all your versions, all seasons, all parts of you. I should have cared for you with the same care I tried to receive from others. I should have loved you more. Unconditionally and entirely, not only when I waited to be whole first, not knowing you were the missing part to make me complete.

Love yourself

Love yourself enough to stand up for yourself and what you believe in. Love yourself enough to speak your mind and be a voice for your pain. Love yourself enough to place boundaries and say no. Love yourself enough to walk away from places that I've hurt you and love yourself harder to never come back to these exact same places. Love yourself enough to be accountable for your mistakes and forgiving too. Love yourself enough to take care of yourself each day. Love yourself enough to identify what love shouldn't be. Love yourself a little harder every day so you know what it feels like to be loved, so when someone tries to give you half of what you deserve, you'll know you deserve better. Love yourself enough to know that you are deserving of being loved.

The moment I fell back in love with myself

Love followed me everywhere

CHAPTER 3

"And still... I love"

"I still believe in love because of the way I love"

To my heart

To my heart,
I set you free.
Let you feel that it's real.
Let you know that you're still providing,
Let you know that you're abiding.
To my heart,
I set you free.
Go, leave that cage of yours.
See what this life has in store.
And if tomorrow never comes,
You'll know you've lived till your last beating.
Honey, it is okay, if you have to bleed,
Let it be complete bloodshed.
If you have to break, let it shatter.
If you have to love,
Let it be almost like Icarus loved the sun,
Like Camoes loved his book,
Like God loved his son.

It is okay to be terrified to start again and reprogram your mind and heart to be open to love. Or to unlearn all the barriers that you created around it because healing isn't linear and nor is love.

Vulnerability held me by the throat with both its hands and love got stuck in between it, without knowing whether to throw it up or swallow it. Except before you notice it, it bursts inside of you.

It is one of those things that you don't see coming and before you know it is already here, making you laugh from morning to night, offering their time and attention, talking about desires, goals and the life of their dreams. Before you realise it, it is there, placing you right in between the lips of the future that you yearn so much to kiss. Not realising that the day is no longer day without their good morning texts, and night is no longer night without their good night kisses.

Love arrives with no warning and, before you realise it, you're in the kitchen holding a recipe book on your left hand and a wooden spoon on your right hand trying to learn how to cook all the favourite dishes that they like to eat. Before you realise it, you're wearing that red silk dress you've kept hidden in your wardrobe because they said it looked sexy on you. Before you notice, the wounds you took so long to heal fear opening up again. And it is frightening to believe that the past will not replicate itself in the present. To trust that love came for an extended visit. To trust that this time, it decided to stay.

That this time, love chose you. To trust that you're giving someone all the necessary tools to hurt you, but they will use them to destroy all the barriers you've built around love instead.

Be patient they say,

but I have this urge

this feeling pulsating

this tender spot wanting to be touched

Be patient they say

Sometimes I feel like I am in this rush

but how soon is too soon?

How long is too long?

And how much is too much?

My heart aches for you

don't make me wait for too long

You deserve to be loved fully, entirely,

exclusively, truly, unconditionally, loved.

Not in halves, not in uncertainty or reluctancy

Wholeheartedly.

Loved.

Has anyone ever told you about the loneliness that also comes when you learn how to love yourself? When you honour your boundaries, your desires and worth. When you are too cautious about who to let in. Sometimes, loneliness makes you want to open that door or leave it ajar because some nights you'll need more than self-love. You sit and wonder, If I am whole and complete, then why do I still feel this emptiness? If I love my own company, where does this solitude come from?

The truth is, some nights, self-love isn't enough. We all need love, and it is okay to admit it. They say it takes a village, we all crave a sense of belonging, a community. Sisterhood and brotherhood. No one was born to be alone. There are nights when self-love isn't enough. We need ears that can hear what our silence says.

Someone to just sit next to you and talk about anything and everything. Someone to ask you how you really feel inside. To laugh at your jokes, sympathise with your tears, to encourage you and help you face your fears. Someone to get drunk with and dance to your favourite playlist. Someone to hold you and pray with you. Everyone says "you should love yourself first" and I do, but sometimes self-love alone isn't enough. Sometimes you want to share that love with someone else too.

When the world is crashing down on you
And there's no strength to get up from the ruins
It's that hand that grabs you
That hand that holds you
Fingers that take your hair out of face
A smile that reassures you that you'll get back to yourself
It's that voice that calms you down
That tells you at the end you'll be okay
While you mourn for the ones who've left
You have to be to grateful for the ones who stay
That hand that soothe your tears
While you go through things you don't tell anyone else about
Oh thank God for friendships that hold you together
That make sure you still eat even when your stomach is tangled
When you're in so much pain to digest anything
It's those who sit in silence with you
 That share your pain like their own
That makes you leave your bed when all you want is to die in it
The ones that never leave even when you ask them to
Oh thank God for that hand that does not let you go

-   *friendship*

When love returns

I hope it arrives gently

I hope it provides you safety

And reassurance without needing it

I hope it shows you

Nothing is ever lost in this world

It will feel like everything you've lost

Coming back to you tenfold.

Still I love

You were the beginning I never saw coming and I was the end
to all your searching

Walls of safety

There was a wall I built so high designed with labyrinths
And security systems in every corner of my heart.
I installed cameras, control systems
And maintenance in every curvature of my body.
And even then, you were able to infiltrate inside me
Like a virus that my innate immune system
was not able to attack.
You removed that wall brick by brick
 Finding the way out of the labyrinth I created in my mind.
Little by little, I started turning the cameras off
Shutting the security systems down
calming down my heart and mind
And creating in you a bridge of love
Destroying my inner comfort zone
Knowing that on the other side of the bridge
There was a love and arms of safety
that I was assuredly ready to cross for

A heart attached to nothing is a safe heart

But I don't want to be safe

I want danger

I want passion

I want love

I want you.

Perfect

If you are looking for perfection
Do not come for me
I was carved in a unique way
Delicate, exquisite, perfectly flawed.
If real is not what you seek
I'd recommend you to keep me at bay
Sweet as honey with a salty aftertaste
stifling summer night heat
Or an autumn breeze
But my love will always be at
the right climate for you
 Will always be unconditional for you
Because I never look for perfection
I look for love and loyalty
I do not seek for the best in people
I seek for the truth, even if it isn't as pretty as it seems
If you are looking for perfection
Do not come for me
Nobody loves and walks away unscathed
But I promise you it will be an unforgettable walk.

Spiral

Life is a unfathomable spiral

It will hurt, it will break

You will start healing

You will find joy in between

You will learn from it

You will heal

You will love

You might hurt again

You might break again

but you'll heal.

And you'll love

Again & again & again.

You don't need to be fully healed to be deserving of love

All versions of you deserve loving too

All parts of you are deserving of grace.

Still I love

Handle me with care
I need someone who allows me to stay soft
I lived my whole life having to harden my heart
to show up strong

Thousand metres deep

All I ever wanted was to fall in love
Fall a thousand metres deep
Skyscraper tall
Wrap myself around your finger
Thinking about eternity with you
Slow dancing to our favourite playlist.

All I ever wanted was to fall in love
A thousand metres deep
Skyscraper tall
A love that gives and takes in equal measure
A love that consumes me and makes me wonder
Where have you been all this time?

All I ever wanted was to fall in love
A love sets my heart ablaze
A love that sets my soul on fire
And you're the only one that can either
Ignite or extinguish it.
I want to reek of love
Drive myself crazy in love

I want pancakes and kisses for breakfast
Texts saying you missed me already at noon
Love promises and your body intertwined
with mine till we fall back asleep
The world revolving just around me and you
Traffic lights stuck in green for us

All I ever wanted was to fall in love
Fall a thousand metres deep.

Fill me with love

Love spills from my lips like honey
Drips down my chin onto my shirt
Stains every layer of my skin with its sweetness
It seeps from my fingertips
Staining all these pages

So I let it stain, let it soak in
With everything I once thought it was out of reach
When love invades you from within
You transboard, you spill it everywhere
Contaminating everything you touch

Filling every crevice
Coursing through veins like a raging river
Invading every thought, every action
Leaving no stone unturned
Passion pulsing, powerful and pleasing,
Moments melt into memories meeting
Before you know it,
 It has already consumed you
You'll love it here

Love

They say love has no limits
It has no borders
No timezones
No barriers

Mine does not rush
It always awaits
With no space for confusion
Or fears nor doubts

Love is fire, but it doesn't burn
It is intense but doesn't suffocate
It's deep, but doesn't drown

Mine are promises that are kept
Conversations that stimulate
Words that reaffirm, that praise, that kiss
And that touch where your hands cannot touch yet

Love is acceptance, it is adaptation
It is accepting the highs, as well as the lows
It is kissing the smooth and the scarred
The whole and the broken

Mine has a smile that always pushes my shyness out
It has arms that hold, that protect, that comfort
 That guides to where the future can take us

Love has no translation even with all these languages
There is no direction or entry, even with all these exits
Although mine has guided me to you

Still I love

Love is giving without expecting anything in return
It is to feel that you make everything you touch better
Love is being upset because you didn't tell me
 that you arrived home well
Love is wanting to give everything,
even when you have nothing

It's losing my sleep because you lost yours
It is to find everything that I once had lost
and be able to call it mine

They say love has no limits
It has no borders
No time zones
No barriers

Mine is everything you are
and what I hope we can build.

butter

Your touch dismantles me
I melt like butter in between your fingers
Bring them to my mouth
I have been longing for your kiss
Hold me close and don't let go
Tell me how much you love me so
Your fingertips dance across my skin
Tracing every inch of my being
Awaking all my senses
Warming me to my core
Breaking down all my defences
Leaving me breathless and begging for more
Your touch dismantles me
I melt like butter in between your fingers

Still you

The fervid touch of your lips pressed on my neck, I still feel it
Stumbling over my words but I still want you unquestionably
Eyes that always find mine as I stray further from your sight,
With all the flaws I refuse to see in you, I still want you
That white house with blue shutters, yes, I still remember it
Tracing the lines of your palm, and every one draws me back to you

Forevermore

That gentle soft love
holding me like a china cup
but firmly when needed to
I want that space in between the wanting and the giving
the anticipation sending shivers down my spine
the long conversations past midnight
I want the back of my hand kissed at red lights
your presence passionately lingering
everything you touch, turning into love
a love beyond sight, beyond touch, beyond the superficial
above everything I thought love ever was
I want that space between the now and forever
I want you forevermore.

Lucky

How did I get so lucky?
To have find you right under my nose
But had been looking for you everywhere else
The love you seek is seeking you, I suppose
How did I get so lucky?
To have fallen deeply in love
I haven't gotten up ever since
I have longed for a love that would not only catch me
But also set me free
The type of love that it's so giving but also so selfish
That offers you the best of both worlds
An adventure of all sorts
Otherworldly, that transcends anything I ever lived
How lucky I am to love you
How lucky to find you here

Sometimes I hold my tongue
Other times I'm too clumsy with my words
A totally mess of syllables
Should I say what I feel
Or should I feel what I say
As those three words slipped through between my lips
And I could sense you smiling from within
I thought to myself what a mess
But for the first time in a long time
I finally said what I felt and
I knew you felt what I said.

-   *I love you*

need you

need you to lay my head on
when the world feels heavy
how do you make everything so light
need you not as a necessity
need you not as a form of completion
more of an addition, better as multiplication
but tell me how all my calculations sum to you
I don't need someone who completes me
I need someone who gives me freedom to evolve and grow
need you to remind me sometimes I have to let go
sometimes I have to let in
for my free and self-sufficient mind
this "strong independent" soul also wants
to be soft and dependent
also wants to need and be needed
also wants to love and be loved
need you as a reminder that healthy love reciprocates

I chased the chasing

I craved the craving

I wanted the wanting

I loved the loving

Wish someone had told me

I didn't have to chase to be chosen

I spent too many nights writhing in pain
from relationships that left me
broken and stained
I thought love was supposed to hurt
that pain was just part of the package
But now I see
that love can be gentle
that it doesn't have to leave me
bruised and blind-sided
Love can be tender too
Sometimes bittersweet
but I will choose to taste every bit of it

Stay where your mind finds peace
Stay where your heart finds love
Stay where your soul finds home

More

I want eternity and longevity
Now and forevermore
To choose you every day
And keep choosing you thousands of days more.
 Live this life and many others with you,
A hundred lifetimes and I would still choose you
Because only this one isn't enough for me
if loving you is all I have
then I want more of you

How much easier would loving be if we communicated more. If we opened up more, demonstrated more, felt more, with no restraints, with nothing to hold back. How much easier life would be if we took it as how it is and not as how we perceive it to be. No impulse actions and jumping straight to conclusions. I don't want to fall asleep mad at you, guilt trip or deliver loud silent treatments pretending that it doesn't hurt both of us. How much easier would it be if we could just sit here and breathe a bit longer than usual, clear our minds and stop this impulse to run away from each other every time something goes wrong. And all these choices, do you think it gets easier with the next one if all you do is keep running away? How much easier would loving be if we faced the consequences a relationship brings. Nobody wants to touch the wound, but ignoring it won't make it heal easier but together, I promise, it can get easier.

You don't need to beg anyone to love you properly. The person who truly loves you will go above and beyond. They will travel between heaven and earth to make you happy. They will care for you, they will listen to understand you better, they will choose to love you better. They will put you first with no excuses. If they truly love you, you will know and if they don't you'll know better.

I wonder if you ever get tired of running through my mind
From the very first moment I set my eyes on you
You've showed me so many different ways one can bloom
I never knew love could ever feel like this
Missing you even when you hadn't have left
Anticipating your touch every time you are near
My heart colliding with my mind
This ecstasy, so thrilling but also so peaceful
I want to kiss you till my lips go numb
I want your body to merge with mine
Be stuck inside your skin
Tell me, do you want me like I want you?
Tell me how far you want to go
And we can go further
Tell me how deep you want to go
And we can go deeper
Tell me how much you want this love
And I'm a keeper

Thank you for loving me entirely
Even the parts of me that aren't easy to love
Even when I am falling apart
And putting each piece back together
For being kind to the parts of me that are still learning
Kissing the parts that hurt the most, when needed the most
Thank you for being patient with my growing pains
As I outgrow the parts of me you once knew
As I deconstruct what I thought it was, with what it is
Thank you for bringing reassurance to my anxiety
As we take down these walls
these walls I built around my heart
and you still found way to make it through
running through my veins, pulsating, ruminating
taking your time touching
every part of me I once thought
was dormant, forever asleep
And if this is lucid dreaming
don't ever wake me up
Let me love you through thick and thin
through the highs and lows
Through every moment
Through every crack in the heart
broken and healed
For when we're at our best,
And when we're at our worst
I will hold you tightly
I will love you each day slightly more
In every moment, in every way,
trust me to love you with all I can
let me love you with all I am

Erise Amado

There are hugs that feel like home

Hug me harder, hold a little bit longer

Let me take refuge in you.

Still I love

Everyone else made me see the wrongs from the past, you made me see how right our future could be.

How he speaks to me

He gazes intensely while speaking,
Studying me like a dictionary,
Every inch of me from A to Z.
Words escape effortlessly through his lips,
Poetry to my ears, and oxytocin in my head.
A voice that hypnotises,
Making a simple hello sound like "come here".
A low pitch that vibrates to parts of me he is yet to meet.
Only he knows how to pronounce my name the best,
For when he does tell me to come,
I am already coming undressed.

If you leave me softer, lighter, happier than I once was
and if these moments ever slip from between my fingers
And I cannot grasp them, I hope to still relive them
I hope to still find peace in knowing
that at least love was gentle this time while passing through me

Rainforest

Dusky brown eyes gazing at me,
you smell like fresh soil after a rainfall,
musky and sweet.
Sharp, fresh aroma of ozone,
Electrifying me from my flesh to my bone.
You walk like you have thousands of species dwelling inside you,
Every step is so different, kaleidoscopical.
Your accent is so foreign, so tropical.
Hair strands entwined around my fingers
As roots deeply caved into the ground.
Your body is a forest fire, igniting everything earthbound.
Waterfall running from places it shouldn't run
A mind so persuasive, makes a man commit manslaughter.
The mother nature in between your legs that makes mouths water.

Intimacy

Intimacy lies in the ability to touch me without the need of pressing skin against one another, noticing when a smile is semi-crooked or understanding me when no words are uttered. It is that silence that you hear so well. It is to be deeply rooted in one's mind. So connected that there's no plug to turn it off. It is in the call past midnight and when you finally find the good in your goodbyes. It is the vulnerability in strength, closeness even when apart, safety when off guard.
It is feeling so comfortable, like at home, that at times you've seen me naked, felt almost as if I was covered.

Your voice itself undresses me
your hands are itching for their turn

"Red laced lingerie, matte, satin or vinyl? Make a wish." You look at me across the room, with a hint of mischief in your eyes, hands itching, licking your lips in anticipation. Anticipation is not your forte, and my ego feasts of it. I've got you wrapped around my finger, even if it is hard for you to admit. *"Come here."* You say.

Your thumb contours the fullness of my lips that unabashedly beseech for a taste of your skin. Your index tilts my chin up. *"Where's my kiss?"* You ask. I suck the lime and strawberry taste out of you. *"Pour me some of that."* Instead, you kiss me intensively, urgently, and scoop me up in your arms to the bed. Switching the power back to you, like you always do.

I guess you're the one that has me wrapped around your finger, and you know it too. You take both my hands and place them above my head. Mouth against my neck. Sucking. Licking. Marking territory. Fingertips slide down through my body like a brush painting a canvas, searching for places to fit in, to thereafter tear apart. My body stretches like an easel, trembling for art. Here I am, entirely yours to satiate and wallow. You make your fingers dance for me, and my body always follows. Warm, sweet nectar, dripping down your fingers. Let me clean them with my mouth, I love kissing you when your lips taste like me. Hands grip my thighs, while your tongue writes our future in cursive in between my legs. Making music out of me. Reading me without a script. No wonder I always fall for the artist.

Climaxing to you feels like that very first draft, that very first sketch of my pencil, that very first bar, that very first note on a piano, that very first verse that I want to continue reading over and over again. Perfecting it over and over again. Contemplating it over and over again. So you do it over and over again, waiting for the masterpiece to manifest out of me.

Thank you for showing me that I can turn a man into a volcano
and watch him erupt.
I loved to watch you explode.

Men like him

"Come closer", he demanded. I just stood there, static. He moisturised his lips with the tip of his tongue, took a few steps towards me, his arms encaging me, joints cracking against the wall. He approximated until the air I was breathing became the air he was exhaling.
My mother warned me about men like him. Men like him are natural catastrophes, they destroy everything they touch. yet they have the competence of touching you without the need of contact.

How do you do that? Explain to me. How do you touch me without touching me? Sending waves of chills from the layers of my skin to the superficial of my spine. You electrify me. Taking my body as hostage every time that you attempt to negotiate with my mind, you exhaust me.

Guzzling the remnants of my decency, you drain me. Leaving me with lips parting imploring for a kiss, hands to unravel every pore of my skin. Men like him have the power to pick you up and pin you down, to tie your legs and demand you to walk, the type of men that makes "hello" sound like "come here".

Men like him feed you lies, making them taste so good you think that that is the best thing you ever put in your mouth. You forget what truth tastes like. His thumb contoured my lips which finally parted to meet his, but those lips never came to meet mine.

"What do you want me to do to you?" He whispers into my ears, my body squirms. The anticipation was my defeat. I was into a trance.

He looks at me like an artist appreciating his masterpiece, as something that is placed into your palms, yet you can never quite touch. How is that possible? When his mouth is tensely closed, but I feel it everywhere. His tongue twirling everywhere. I imagine his hands grasping my thighs. Lips transforming my refusal into acceptance. All my exits into an entrance. And I let him undress me, shedding the layers of my pride one by one. His fingers sinking into my flesh.

There's no request for permission, he just makes his way throughout my body waiting for the answer to come out from between my legs. And I let him savour me. And I let him invade me. My anatomy swallowing his. Breaking through the doors of my being, welcoming him to the warmth of my walls, in my head, welcoming him home.
My mother warned me about men like him. Men like him are natural catastrophes, they destroy everything they touch, and here I am, imploring you to destroy me.

This. This is what men like him do to you.

This, this is how you touch me without touching me.

Canvas

His fingers reach the pencil, and I let a smile as a crescendo
escape from my lips.
Confusedly mesmerised, my mind is captivated by his.
Every line he draws I see myself on it, a white canvas waiting
for him to touch me, waiting for him to stain me ...
And he lets the pencil swing between his fingers, and I permit
my tongue to swirl against the walls of my mouth. I wanted
him there, exactly there. I observed him hold the canvas firmly
as he should've held me, risks and scribbles flooding on the
now stained rectangle and I wished to be there, exactly there.
My eyes fixed on him, and his eyes fixed on his art. So much
beauty to contemplate, without even knowing where to start.
And I wished to be his canvas, and be there, exactly there.
Allowing his fingertips to contour my lines, allowing the graph-
ite of his pencil to bring the fervour to my thighs. Hazel eyes
fixed on mine, still, an unfinished canvas entirely at his will.
He moisturises his lips with the tip of his tongue, and I let him
finish.

"What should we call this piece? I think I finished it," he asks.
Let me think about it while you finish me.

Meu amor (my love)

Meu amor, let me tell you
There are lips that dream of kisses like yours
Ears crave your moans at night
Eyes hunt for the sight of you in the morning
Tongues would kill for a taste of you in the afternoon
Nostrils quest everywhere for a scent of you
Skin longs for the touch of your fingertips
Necks have been waiting for a print of your teeth
Thighs anticipate the grasp of your hands
My body is a language only your tongue understands
Meu amor, I always thought you knew,
Every inch of me, craves every inch of you

"I want to build a home out of you

where I have no fear of becoming homeless"

Distance taught me that being close has nothing to do with proximity when you are so present in me. Sometimes I feel that I touch you, other times, I feel that I hear you in rooms that you never entered.
I carry you everywhere, and I don't even realise it.

"I wanted you here
but you're there
with your face buried
on your pillow
and that pillow
doesn't even know
how lucky it is."
-   *the distance*

I leave traces of you in every love poem
I hope you run your fingers over each verse you read
I want every word to touch you how you touch me
To make you feel how you make me feel

The serenity, the synchronicity
The peace you bring to my chaotic heart
The urge to love you with no rush
Intense but gentle
Mad yet sane

I leave traces of you in every verse
I want to spread our love in all these pages.
May all the bookstores be filled with a part of you.
A part of us.
Let everyone know that a love like ours exists.

Our lips kissed goodbye,
But my body did not want to part from you.
"The uber is waiting" they told me.
But I just wanted time to wait for me.
To rewind for us.
I just wanted the world to freeze for us.
The noise to quieten down for us.
So you could listen to what I had to say
But wasn't brave enough to tell you.

    - *I love you*

Gravity

I keep gravitating towards you
Newton hasn't explained this law yet
Even Picasso couldn't have pictured this
inside his creative genius mind
Perhaps we should ask Aristotle
but you have never been a fan of philosophy or religion
I cannot ask you to ask God or tell you about the times
I prayed for you before I even knew you existed
Arms that held me before I knew they would be open
Love that had loved me before I knew this type of love existed
I have driven myself to exhaustion of missing
something I never had
Would I be kissing you for the first time?
Will I be making love to you for the first time?
If my fingers seem to remember where to touch
If my mouth seems to know exactly how to please you
If my body has created a memory of you and has
Been clenching for the feeling of you.
I keep gravitating towards you.
A magnet I cannot repel from
I'd swore I have loved you since the beginning of time.
I have been yours before I even knew you'd be mine.

Still I love

I want to be loved eloquently.
With no measurements of affection
With no limits on touch
I want your hands everywhere.
Curious, careful, caring
Capriciously running through my body.

I want to be stuck in that smile in the middle of the kiss.
In that anticipation before the touch.
I want to be stuck with you.

With no mind games
With no wars over who feels the most.
Or who hurt the other the most.
No hot-headed decisions and regrets
Without jumping to conclusions just because
we think that those who remain silent consent.

Talk to me. I want a love that speaks for itself.
But I also want you to tell me about it.
With no comparisons.
With no room for doubt.

Transparent and clear as water
That flows and nourishes everything it touches.
I want to be stuck in the early hours of Sunday.
When we undress our secrets, doubts,
Dreams, and our achievements
Drinking your favourite wine.

I want to be loved eloquently, out loud,
But also in between moans and whispers.
When I sing your name in your ear.

I just want to be loved eloquently.
To have your lap in the middle of my unrest.
A place to lay my head in the midst of my torments.
I want to be stuck between you and our love forever
I want to be stuck with you.

Still I love

I love the version you bring in me

What is love to you?

Love is…easy, it is meant to be easy, light and transparent,
healthy, not a jigsaw puzzle. It just flows, it grows, it empowers
and allows you to be. It is exciting, it is intense but never rushes,
it awaits.

Perhaps love is wanting to give you
flowers while you can still smell them.
Or the sweetness of my lips while you can taste them.
And the reassurance in my words and in my actions.

To learn your love languages and everything in between them.
Undress all my insecurities while you kiss them,
Perhaps it is the arms of safety that are always ready to catch me.
That embraces and protects me.
This energy pulling me towards you,
And I can't get enough of you.

Maybe love is to remove all the barriers,
Every wall and build bridges.
It is forgiveness and acceptance.
In moments that I can't forgive myself.

It's that 3 am drive that you do when I am hungry
That presence when I feel lonely
It is companionship
That ted talk you give me when I am not motivated.
The nights you stay up late with me working on my projects.

Maybe love is when you love my beautiful and my ugly.
When you make me feel like the sexiest woman
That has ever walked on Earth
The most beautiful that you ever contemplated

Perhaps love is when you stay over every time
self-doubt visits me.
Praying with me.
Taking my makeup off when I fall asleep
Holding me together when I fall apart

Maybe love is the better version of me
That is taking time to build
Because I love taking my time building it with you.

Love is raw yet delicate.
Handcrafted,
Created
God-made

Oh tell me,
What is love to you?
Because
To me
Love is you.

Plot Twist

After all the cracks I have opened
All the mazes I have escaped
Every wound I have healed
Where the solitude invaded

After all the places I have been
Every skin I ever kissed
Every soul I ever touched
And all the bullets I have missed

After every soul that has ever left me
And those that have lost me
Every lesson I have learned
Just to teach others how to love me

Who would have foreseen
That love would find me here
Who would have thought
I am my favourite plot twist

Still I love

ABOUT THE AUTHOR

Erise Amado is a poet and content creator from Sao Tome and Principe islands, based in London. After years of sharing her writing and thoughts online from her own journey through self-love, growth, healing and love she decided to put them into a poetry collection. She hopes her words bring the same peace and reassurance that writing does for her. She hopes her experiences inspire others to still feel, to still heal, to still love.

instagram.com/eriseamado

Still I love

Printed in Great Britain
by Amazon

25008435R00117